OUR ULTIMATE
HOPE

7 [...]
REN[...] [...]OUL

MAX LUCADO

THOMAS NELSON
Since 1798

Published in Nashville, Tennessee, by Thomas Nelson. Thomas Nelson is a registered trademark of HarperCollins Christian Publishing, Inc.

Thomas Nelson titles may be purchased in bulk for educational, business, fundraising, or sales promotional use. For information, please e-mail SpecialMarkets@ThomasNelson.com.

ISBN 978-1-4002-1211-8 (eBook)

ISBN 978-1-4002-1210-1 (SC)

Printed in the United States of America

18 19 20 21 22 LSC 6 5 4 3 2 1

Contents

The Eternal Promise

There is now no condemnation for
those who are in Christ Jesus.

—ROMANS 8:1

New York City.

If you want a view of the skyline, visit the Brooklyn Bridge.

For entertainment go to Broadway.

Looking for inspiration? Tour the Statue of Liberty.

Like to shop? The stores on Fifth Avenue await your credit card.

But if you want to be depressed, utterly overwhelmed, and absolutely distraught, take a cab to the corner of the Avenue of the Americas and West Forty-Fourth Street and spend a few moments in the presence of the US National Debt Clock. The sign is twenty-five feet wide, weighs fifteen hundred pounds, and uses 306 bulbs to constantly, mercilessly, endlessly declare the US debt and each family's share. The original clock wasn't built to run backward, but that feature has seldom been needed. Plans to install an updated model that can display some quadrillion dollars have been discussed.[1] If debt were a tidal wave, according to this sign the undertow is going to suck us out to sea.

I'm not an economist; I'm a preacher. But my monetary experience has taught me this: when people owe more than they own, expect trouble.

Again, I'm not an economist. I'm a preacher, which may explain the odd question that occurred to me as I pondered the debt clock. What if heaven had one of these? A marquee that measured not our fiscal debt but our spiritual one? Scripture often refers to sin in financial terminology. Did Jesus not teach us to pray, "Forgive us our debts" (Matthew 6:12)? If sin is a debt, do you and I have a dot matrix trespass counter in heaven? Does it click at each infraction?

We lie. *Click.*

We gossip. *Click.*

We demand our way. *Click.*

We doze off while reading a Lucado book. *Click, click, click.*

Talk about depressing. A financial liability is one matter, but a spiritual one? The debt of sin has a serious consequence. It separates us from God.

> Your iniquities have separated
>   you from your God;
> your sins have hidden his face from you,
> so that he will not hear. (Isaiah 59:2)

The algebra of heaven reads something like this: heaven is a perfect place for perfect people, which leaves us in a perfect mess. According to heaven's debt clock we owe more than we could ever repay. Every day brings more sin, more debt, and more questions like this one: "Who will deliver me?" (Romans 7:24 NKJV).

The realization of our moral debt sends some people into a frenzy of good works. Life becomes an unending quest to do enough, be better, accomplish more. A pursuit of piety. We attend church, tend to the sick, go on pilgrimages, and go on fasts. Yet deep within is the gnawing fear, *What if having done all that, I've not done enough?*

Other people respond to the list not with activity but unbelief. They throw up their hands and walk away exasperated. No God would demand so much. He can't be pleased. He can't be satisfied. He must not exist. If he does exist, he is not worth knowing.

Two extremes. The legalist and the atheist. The worker desperate to impress God. The unbeliever convinced there is no God. Can you relate to either of the two? Do you know the weariness that comes from legalism? Do you know the loneliness that comes from atheism?

What do we do? Are despair and disbelief the only options?

No Condemnation

No one loved to answer that question more than the apostle Paul, who said, "There is now no condemnation for those who are in Christ Jesus" (Romans 8:1).

How could he say this? Had he not seen the debt we owe? He'd certainly seen his own. Paul entered the pages of Scripture as Saul, the self-professed Pharisee of all Pharisees and the most religious man in town. But all his scruples and law keeping hadn't made him a better person.

He was bloodthirsty and angry, determined to extinguish anything and everyone Christian.

His attitude began to change on the road to Damascus. That's when Jesus appeared to him in the desert, knocked him off his high horse, and left him sightless for three days. Paul could see only one direction: inward. And what he saw he did not like. He saw a narrow-minded tyrant. During his time of blindness God gave him a vision that a man named Ananias would restore his sight. So, when Ananias did, Paul "got up and was baptized" (Acts 9:18).

Within a few days he was preaching about Christ. Within a few years he was off on his first missionary journey. Within a couple of decades, he was writing the letters we still read today, each one of which makes the case for Christ and the cross.

We aren't told when Paul realized the meaning of grace. Was it immediately on the Damascus road? Or gradually during the three-day darkness? Or after Ananias restored his sight? We aren't told. But we know that Paul got grace. Or grace got Paul. Either way, he embraced the improbable offer that God would make us right with him through Jesus Christ. Paul's logic followed a simple outline:

Our debt is enough to sink us.
God loves us too much to leave us.
So, God has found a way to save us.

The Problem

Paul began his case for Christ by describing our problem: "For all have sinned and fall short of the glory of God" (Romans 3:23). We haven't met the standard God set. We were intended to bear the nature of God. To speak, act, and behave the way he speaks, acts, and behaves. To love as he loves. To value what he values. To honor those he honors. This is the glorious standard God has set. We have failed to meet it. Jesus, on the other hand, succeeded. "Christ never sinned" (2 Corinthians 5:21 NLV).

What a remarkable statement! Not once did Jesus turn right when he was supposed to turn left. He never stayed silent when he was supposed to speak, or spoke when he was supposed to stay silent. He was "tempted in every way, just as we are—yet he did not sin" (Hebrews 4:15). He was the image of God twenty-four hours a day, seven days a week.

When it comes to the standard, he is the standard. To be sinless is to be like Jesus.

But who can be?

We may have occasional moments of goodness and perform deeds of kindness, but who among us reflects the image of God all day every day? Paul couldn't find anyone. "As it is written: 'There is no one righteous, not even one; there is no one who understands; there is no one who seeks God'" (Romans 3:10–11).

People often bristle at the message of these verses. They take offense at its allegation. No one is righteous? No one seeks God? And then they produce their résumés of righteousness. They pay taxes. They love their families. They avoid addiction. They give to the poor. They seek justice for the oppressed. Compared to the rest of the world, they are good people.

Ah, but herein lies the problem. Our standard is not the rest of the world. Our standard is Christ. Compared to Christ, we, well . . . Can you hear the debt clock?

Sometime back I took up swimming for exercise. I didn't buy a Speedo, but I did buy some goggles, went to a pool, and gave it a go. Over the weeks I gradually progressed from a tadpole to a small frog. I'm not much to look at, but I can get up and down the lane. In fact, I was beginning to feel pretty good about my progress.

So good, in fact, that when Josh Davis invited me to swim with him, I accepted. You remember Josh Davis, three-time gold medalist in the Atlanta Olympics. His waist size is my thigh size. Half of his warm-up is my entire workout. He is as comfortable in a swimming lane as most of us are in a cafeteria lane.

So when he offered to give me some pointers, I jumped in the pool. (A pool, incidentally, that bears the name Josh Davis Natatorium.) After all, I had two months of swimming experience under my belt . . . Senior Olympics? Who knows? So, with Josh in his lane and me next to him in mine, he suggested, "Let's swim two laps and see how fast you go." Off I went. I gave it all I had. I was surprised at the finish to see that he had touched the wall only seconds before me. I felt pretty good about myself. I half expected to see photographers and endorsers gathered on the edge of the pool.

"Have you been here long?" I panted.

"Just a few seconds."

"You mean I finished only a few seconds behind you?"

"That's right."

Whoa . . . Forget Senior Olympics. I'm thinking world-record holder. But then Josh added, "There was one difference. While you swam one lap, I swam three." (I suspect he actually swam four.)

Josh raised the bar. He displayed swimming at the highest level.

On a minute scale he did in the pool what Jesus did for humanity.

Jesus demonstrated what a godly life looks like.

The Solution

So what are we to do? He is holy; we are not. He is perfect; we are not. His character is flawless; ours is flawed. A yawning canyon separates us from God. Might we hope that God will overlook it? He would, except for one essential detail. He is a God of justice. If he does not punish sin, he is not just. If he is not just, then what hope do we have of a just heaven? The next life would be occupied by sinners who found a loophole, who skirted the system. Yet if God punishes us for our sin, then we are lost. So, what is the solution? Again, we turn to Paul for the explanation:

> What does Scripture say? "Abraham believed God, and it was credited to him as righteousness."
> Now to the one who works, wages are not credited as a gift but as an obligation. However, to the one who does not work but trusts God who justifies the ungodly, their faith is credited as righteousness. (Romans 4:3–5)

To credit something is to make payment for it. I have a credit card. If I were to write a check to pay the balance on the card, the debt on the card would be removed, and I would be credited a zero balance. I would have no debt. No outstanding payment. No obligation. None whatsoever.

According to Paul, God has done the same with our spiritual debt. He presents Abraham as an example of a grace recipient. Yes, Abraham from 2000 BC! Abraham had not a credit-card debt but a spiritual debt. He had sinned. He was a good man, I am certain, but not good enough to live debt-free. His debt clock had abundant clicks.

Every time he cursed his camel. *Click.*
Every time he flirted with a handmaiden. *Click.*
Every time he wondered where in the world
    God was leading him and if God knew
    where in the world he was headed. *Click.*
    Click. Click.

But for all the bad things Abraham did, there
was one good thing he chose to do. He believed.
He put his faith in God. And because he believed,
a wonderful, unspeakably great thing happened
to his debt clock.

It was returned to zero!

"Abraham believed God, and it was credited
to him as righteousness." God's promise to
Abraham was salvation by faith. God's promise to
you and me is salvation by faith. Just faith.

God sacrificed Jesus on the altar of the world
    to clear that world of sin. Having faith in
    him sets us in the clear. God decided on this
    course of action in full view of the public—to
    set the world in the clear with himself
    through the sacrifice of Jesus, finally taking
    care of the sins he had so patiently endured.
    This is not only clear, but it's *now*—this is

current history! God sets things right. He also makes it possible for us to live in his rightness. (Romans 3:25–26 THE MESSAGE)

God never compromised his standard. He satisfied every demand of justice. Yet he also gratified the longing of love. Too just to overlook our sin, too loving to dismiss us, he placed our sin on his Son and punished it there. "God put the wrong on him who never did anything wrong, so we could be put right with God" (2 Corinthians 5:21 THE MESSAGE).

Now we understand the cry of Christ from the cross: "My God, my God, why have you forsaken me?" (Matthew 27:46).

Jesus felt the wrath of a just and holy God.

Wave after wave. Load after load. Hour after hour. He cried out the words of the psalm he would have known since his youth: "Why have you forsaken me?" He felt the separation between his Father and him.

And then when he could scarcely take any more, he cried, "It is finished!" (John 19:30 NASB). His mission was complete.

At the moment of Jesus' death, an unbelievable miracle occurred. "Jesus cried out with a loud voice, and breathed His last. Then the veil of the temple was torn in two from top to bottom" (Mark 15:37–38 NKJV). "The veil separated the people from the temple's Most Holy Place, and it had done so for centuries. According to tradition, the veil—a handbreadth in thickness—was woven of seventy-two twisted plaits, each plait consisting of twenty-four threads. The veil was apparently sixty feet long and thirty feet wide."[2]

We aren't talking about short, delicate drapes. This curtain was a wall made of fabric. The fact that it was torn from top to bottom reveals that the hands behind the deed were divine. God himself grasped the curtain and ripped it in two.

No more!

No more division. No more separation. No more sacrifices. "No condemnation for those who are in Christ Jesus" (Romans 8:1).

> [Jesus] personally carried our sins
> in his body on the cross
> so that we can be dead to sin
> and live for what is right.
> By his wounds
> you are healed.
>
> (1 PETER 2:24 NLT)

Heaven's work of redemption was finished. Christ's death brought new life. Whatever barrier that had separated—or might ever separate—us from God was gone.

Gone is the fear of falling short! Gone is the anxious quest for right behavior. Gone are the nagging questions: Have I done enough? Am I good enough? Will I achieve enough? The legalist finds rest. The atheist finds hope. The God of Abraham is not a God of burdens but a God of rest. He knows we are made of flesh. He knows we cannot achieve perfection. The God of the Bible is the One who says:

> Come to me, all you who are weary and burdened, and I will give you rest. Take my yoke upon you and learn from me, for I am gentle and humble in heart, and you will find rest for your souls. For my yoke is easy and my burden is light. (Matthew 11:28–30)

When you lose your temper with your child, Christ intervenes. "I paid for that." When you tell a lie and all of heaven groans, your Savior speaks up: "My death covered that sin." As you lust over someone's centerfold, gloat over someone's pain, covet someone's success, or cuss someone's mistake, Jesus stands before the tribunal of heaven and points to the blood-streaked cross. "I've already made provision. I've paid that debt. I've taken away the sins of the world."

Karl Barth described grace in this manner:

> On the one side there is God in His glory as Creator and Lord. . . . And on the other side there is man, not merely the creature, but the sinner, the one who exists in the flesh and who in the flesh is in opposition to Him. It is not merely a frontier, but a yawning abyss. Yet this abyss is crossed, not by man, not by both God and man, but only by God. . . . This man does not even know how it comes about or happens to him.[3]

Salvation, from beginning to end, is a work of our Father. God does not stand on a mountain and tell us to climb it and find him. He comes down into our dark valley and finds us. He does not offer to pay all the debt minus a dollar if we'll pay the dollar. He pays every penny. He doesn't offer to complete the work if we will start it. He does all the work, from beginning to end. He does not bargain with us, telling us to clean up our lives so he can help. He washes our sins without our help.

An elderly woman was once asked about the security of her salvation. Though she'd dedicated her life to the Lord, a cynic asked, "How can you be sure? How can you know that after all these years God won't let you sink into hell?"

"He would lose more than I would," she replied. "All I would lose would be my own soul. He would lose his good name."

What a gift God has given you. You've won the greatest lottery in the history of humanity, and you didn't even pay for the ticket! Your soul is secure, your salvation guaranteed. Your name is written in the only book that matters. You're only a few sand grains in the hourglass from a tearless, graveless, painless existence.

This is the message of God, the promise of grace. The declaration Paul preached with unwearied enthusiasm: "What we cannot do, God has done. He justifies us by his grace." Grace is entirely God's. God loving. God stooping. God offering. God caring and God carrying.

———

This is God's version of grace. Is it yours? Don't hurry too quickly past that question. Guilt simmers like a toxin in far too many souls. Do not let it have a place in yours. Before you turn the page, internalize this promise that is written with the crimson blood of Christ: "There is now no condemnation for those who are in Christ Jesus" (Romans 8:1).

No condemnation. Not "limited condemnation," "appropriate condemnation," or "calculated condemnation." That is what people give people. What does God give his children? "No condemnation."

Stand on this promise. Or, better said, take this promise to the clock, your personal debt clock. As you look up at the insurmountable debt you owe, the debt you can never pay, let this promise be declared: "There is now no condemnation for those who are in Christ Jesus."

Your Response

What are you supposed to do with this free gift of grace? Your response is three simple steps: admit, agree, accept.

1. **Admit** that God has not held first place in your life, and ask him to forgive your sins.

   "If we confess our sins to him, he is faithful and just to forgive us our sins and to cleanse us from all wickedness" (1 John 1:9 NLT).

2. **Agree** that Jesus died to pay for your sins and that he rose from the dead and is alive today.

   "If you declare with your mouth, 'Jesus is Lord,' and believe in your heart that God raised him from the dead, you will be saved" (Romans 10:9).

   "Salvation is found in no one else [other than Jesus], for there is no other name under heaven given to mankind by which we must be saved" (Acts 4:12).

3. **Accept** God's free gift of salvation. Don't try to earn it.

   "For it is by grace you have been saved, through faith—and this is not from yourselves, it is the gift of God—not by works, so that no one can boast" (Ephesians 2:8–9).

"To all who received him, he gave the right to become children of God. All they needed to do was to trust him to save them. All those who believe this are reborn!—not a physical rebirth . . . but from the will of God" (John 1:12–13 TLB).

Jesus says, "Here I am! I stand at the door and knock. If anyone hears my voice and opens the door, I will come in" (Revelation 3:20).

With all my heart, I urge you to accept God's destiny for your life. According to the Bible, "Jesus is the only one who can save people. His name is the only power in the world that has been given to save anyone. We must be saved through him!" (Acts 4:12 ERV).

Would you let him save you? This is the most important decision you will ever make. Why don't you give your heart to him right now? **Admit** your need. **Agree** with his work. **Accept** his gift.

Go to God in prayer and tell him, *I am a sinner in need of grace. I believe that Jesus died for me on the cross. I accept your offer of salvation.* It's a simple prayer with eternal results.

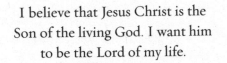

I believe that Jesus Christ is the Son of the living God. I want him to be the Lord of my life.

_____

Signed

_____

Date

Once you've placed your faith in Christ, I urge you to take three steps. You'll find them easy to remember. Just think of these three words, each of which starts with a *b*: *baptism*, *Bible*, and *belonging*.

- **Baptism** demonstrates and celebrates our decision to follow Jesus. The water of baptism symbolizes God's grace. Just as water cleanses the body, so grace cleanses the soul. Jesus said, "Anyone who believes and is baptized will be saved" (Mark 16:16 NCV). When the apostle Paul became a believer, he was asked this question: "Now, why wait any longer? Get up, be baptized, and wash your sins away, trusting in him to save you" (Acts 22:16 NCV). Paul responded by being baptized immediately. You can too.
- **Bible** reading brings us face-to-face with God. God reveals himself to us through his Word by the Holy Spirit. "Let the teaching of Christ live in you richly" (Colossians 3:16 NCV).
- **Belonging** to a church reinforces your faith. A Christian without a church is like a

baseball player without a team or a soldier without an army. You aren't strong enough to survive alone. "You should not stay away from the church meetings, as some are doing, but you should meet together and encourage each other" (Hebrews 10:25 NCV).

These three steps—baptism, Bible reading, and belonging to a church—are essential in your faith.

I pray you'll accept this great gift of salvation. Believe me, this is not only the most important decision you'll ever make, but it's also the greatest soul-altering decision you'll ever make. There's no higher treasure than God's gift of salvation.

If you're not sure where to begin reading the Bible, here are seven days of scriptures and prayers to get you started.

Let Go and Let God

The Promise: I can rest in the
assurance of salvation.

People are counted as righteous, not
because of their work, but because of
their faith in God. (Romans 4:5 NLT)

Blessed is the one whose transgressions are
forgiven, whose sins are covered. (Psalm 32:1)

For it is by grace you have been saved,
through faith—and this is not from
yourselves, it is the gift of God—not by works,
so that no one can boast. (Ephesians 2:8–9)

Everything worthwhile in life takes work.
Getting an A instead of a C on that project.
Earning that promotion at the company. Making
a marriage thrive. We know effort will be

involved, yet we still strive for what we want. So we work, and we stretch, and we pull ourselves up by our bootstraps to achieve success.

And we think we have to do the same for God's approval. Perhaps we need to say a certain number of prayers or serve a few more hours at the soup kitchen just to make things right with God.

But we learn from Abraham one of the greatest promises of Scripture: we are made right with God by faith alone. When we align ourselves with God, we are given a perfect score, a seat at the table, and a place in the family. This is the gift of righteousness by faith.

Maybe you read that and think your faith must be perfect. After all, Abraham is called the father of faith. His faith must have been like a rock, sure and unbending. He must have set the standard for perfect faith. No doubts. No questions. No fear. If anyone had a perfect faith, it must have been Abraham.

That might be easy to believe, but it's not what the Bible says. Let's go back to Genesis 12, which records a covenant the Lord made with Abraham, who was called Abram at the time.

The LORD had said to Abram, "Go from
your country, your people and your father's
household to the land I will show you.

"I will make you into a great nation,
    and I will bless you;
I will make your name great,
    and you will be a blessing.
I will bless those who bless you,
    and whoever curses you I will curse;
and all peoples on earth
    will be blessed through you." (verses 1–3)

This covenant is noteworthy because of what
God offered and what he required. He offered
everything and required *nothing*. All Abraham had
to do to receive it was believe.

But that wasn't so easy. Abraham hadn't
seen what you and I have seen. He didn't have
the benefits of Scripture. He didn't know the
stories of Peter's redemption or Paul's conversion.
He hadn't heard of the virgin birth or the
empty tomb.

Abram was simply told to believe. That
should be simple enough for the man called the
father of faith.

Not quite.

God told Abram to go into the land of Canaan, which was already occupied by bloodthirsty tyrants. And God told Abram he would have a nation of descendants, even though he had no children, and his wife was barren.

Canaan was occupied, the crib was empty, and Abram had a crisis of faith. He asked the Lord, "What can you give me since I remain childless?" (Genesis 15:2). That doesn't exactly sound like a man of great faith.

God responded with a vision and another word. He showed Abram the sky and told him that his offspring would equal the number of the stars in the heavens. Abram could have walked away. He could have laughed off the very idea of having a child in his eighties. But he didn't. "Abram believed the LORD, and he credited it to him as righteousness" (Genesis 15:6).

Looking at Abram's faith, God said, "That's enough. That's all I desire." God granted Abraham a spiritual inheritance not because of his piety or his pedigree but because of his faith. It was a hesitant faith. It was a wavering faith. But it was enough.

The Lord isn't looking for perfect faith. His

promise to Abraham was salvation by faith. His promise to Paul was salvation by faith. God's promise to me and to you is the same.

Gone is the fear of falling short. Gone is the quest to feel right, do right, or know the right things. Gone is the anxiety of uncertainty. We never have to wonder if we've done enough. We are guaranteed our spot in the family of God.

If, after you have accepted the gift of salvation, the old habits of striving and working for God's approval resurface, remember Abraham with his imperfect faith. It was all God desired, and it's all he desires of you.

A Prayer of Promise

God, you are good and righteous and holy. Yet you offer to make me right with you through my bumbling, stumbling faith. I am forever grateful.

Thank you for being enough so I don't have to be. I could never be perfect on my own. And it's such a relief just to rest in the knowledge that you are.

Forgive me when I pick up old habits and

try to earn your love. Remind me that all I need to do is put my faith in you. Let my actions be motivated by what you've already done in my life, a response to your free gift. In Jesus' name, amen.

What Would You Ask of God?

The Promise: I can and will know God.

They will all know me. (Hebrews 8:11)

Without faith it is impossible to please God,
because anyone who comes to him must
believe that he exists and that he rewards
those who earnestly seek him. (Hebrews 11:6)

You will seek me and find me when you seek
me with all your heart. (Jeremiah 29:13)

More than three thousand years ago
Moses pleaded with God on behalf of
the Israelites. "If you don't go with us, no one
will know that you are pleased with me and
with your people. These people and I will be

---

no different from any other people on earth" (Exodus 33:16 NCV). God agreed: "I will do what you ask, because I know you very well, and I am pleased with you" (Exodus 33:17 NCV). Then Moses asked for one more favor.

The prince-turned-shepherd-turned-liberator could ask God for anything. What do you suppose he thought about requesting? He had more than a million irritable Hebrews on his hands. Enemies surrounded them. And the people had yet to claim the promised land.

Surely Moses thought about turning those grumbling Hebrews into sheep. Maybe then they'd be easier to handle. Perhaps he considered a swift salvation from their enemies. Or maybe Moses thought about asking God to send them all straight into the promised land.

All would have been understandable requests. Who could blame Moses? He knew God could do any of them. Moses had witnessed God's power when a staff became a snake and the Red Sea became a red carpet.

So what did Moses request? "Show me your glory" (Exodus 33:18). He forgot about money, passed on the power, and skipped the fountain of youth. Moses wanted one thing: more of God.

He wanted a glimpse of God's glory. He wanted a view of God's greatness because he had great challenges ahead.

You have great challenges too. You're probably not trying to lead a million Hebrews, but you're looking for answers to a million questions. Maybe you have to share a dinner table with grumbling relatives or fight a physical battle just to get out of bed.

Your challenges are great, so you need to understand your great and mighty God. We all need a glimpse of God's glory. We need to see him.

The good news is that he wants to be seen. He even guarantees that a day will come when we will all see the Lord. We'll rest in his radiance and bask in his beauty. In that moment every struggle, every challenge we've ever faced will melt away.

Even now we're invited to gain a glimpse of God and begin to understand who he is. He knows that when we see him, we'll never be the same. Our struggles don't disappear, but we see them in a new light. Our questions may not be immediately answered, but we begin to have new understanding. Our imperfections aren't instantly corrected, but we begin to love with a new heart.

Seeing the face of God changes the face of the worshipper. It did for Moses. When he left the mountain after seeing only a glimpse of God, his face shone so bright that the Hebrews were afraid to come near him. When we witness his majesty and might, we, too, will begin to radiate his love so that those around us can't help but see it.

What is the reward for those who seek God? It is to know God and become more like him.

God will allow himself to be known by all who seek him. Make sure you are one of them.

A Prayer of Promise

Heavenly Father, show me a glimpse of your glory. Your greatness is beyond anything I could ever imagine. Even in the frantic moments of life, open my eyes to your splendor and grace at work around me.

Thank you that you can be known. I cling to the promise that when I seek you, I will find you. Help me pursue you today. Give me a hunger for you alone.

I want to know you more. Forgive me when my mind strays, and help me focus on your glory. In Jesus' name, amen.

What to Do with Fear

The Promise: I do not need to
fear because God is with me.

For he will command his angels concerning you
to guard you in all your ways. (Psalm 91:11)

You are my hiding place;
you will protect me from trouble
and surround me with songs of deliverance.
(Psalm 32:7)

The Lord is with me; I will not be afraid.
What can mere mortals do to me? (Psalm 118:6)

Fearing people is a dangerous trap,
but trusting the Lord means safety.
(Proverbs 29:25 NLT)

God's people are not exempt from violence.
Murderers do not give the godly a pass,

and thieves do not vet victims according to their spiritual résumés. The bloodthirsty and wicked do not skip over the heaven bound.

We are not insulated from pain and heartache. But neither do we need to be intimidated.

Jesus has something to say about this brutal world in which we live. "Do not fear those who kill the body but cannot kill the soul" (Matthew 10:28 ESV). Of all the promises of Christ, this one may be the most honest and unadorned.

He never promises that Christians will be spared persecution or violence. But he firmly assures us that no one can touch our souls. We may not be safe, but we are all secure.

We are secure in God's protection. Secure under God's sovereignty. Secure in God's great promise. "Even though I walk through the darkest valley, I will fear no evil, for you are with me" (Psalm 23:4).

Most of us struggle to process and make sense of the violence and pain we see in the world. We're not alone. Christ's disciples struggled to make sense of their world too. In Matthew 10 Jesus told them to expect scourging, trials, death, hatred, and persecution. That's not exactly the kind of locker room pep talk that rallies the team, is it?

Expecting that kind of treatment, why would they stick around? Perhaps it was because of what they'd witnessed a few weeks earlier. Jesus had faced down the demons inside two exceedingly violent men (Matthew 8). And with a single word, the demons were banished into a herd of pigs.

One word. That's all it took to free those men from bondage and violence. He who sustains the universe with a word is still sovereign over darkness.

Sovereignty may sound like a ten-dollar word, but its definition is pretty simple. Supremacy, dominion, power. It means that God is in control. Nothing happens that is not under his authority. Simply put, you and I will never face anything that God can't handle.

Even—maybe especially—the evil in this world. God can handle it. And because we walk with God, we can face it with courage. Because Jesus wins the battle of good versus evil, you can win the battle of faith versus fear.

God, by his grace, will deposit in you a wellspring of faith and courage. God does not want you or me to live a life marked by trepidation and fear. It simply isn't his will.

We are courageous not because of our muscles but because of our Savior. And courage emerges not because of increased police security but from enhanced spiritual maturity. As we trust in the sovereignty of God and deposit our lives squarely under his protection, we will overcome fear.

We are people of promise, not people of panic. We should not live on edge, always anxious, troubled, looking over our shoulders, unable to rest. This is a time for faith, not fear. It's a time for peace, not panic.

We avoid Pollyanna optimism. After all, no one gains by glossing over the pain of the human existence. But neither do we join the Chicken Little choir parading around saying that the sky is falling.

You belong to neither camp. You are a faithful follower of Christ. You are wide eyed yet unafraid, unterrified by the terrifying. You are the calmest kid on the block, not for lack of bullies, but for faith in your big brother.

You're not foolish or naive. You're careful and mindful. You do not cave in to fear. You walk by faith and remain vigilant in prayer, trusting in God. He has promised to be your shelter and your strength, your guard and your protector.

What more could any of us need in order to face with courage whatever lies ahead?

A Prayer of Promise

You have said, Father, that he who dwells in the secret place of the Most High shall abide under the shadow of the Almighty. You are my refuge. You are my fortress and my God. In you I choose to trust.

You will deliver me from my enemies, and I will take refuge under your wings. Your truth will be my shelter, and I will not be afraid.

You have set your love upon me, Father, and I will trust you. You are good and faithful, and evil runs at the sound of your name. I have nothing to fear, for you are with me. Thank you for your promise of protection and deliverance. In Jesus' name, amen.

When Nothing Goes Right

The Promise: God can be trusted
with every outcome.

In all things God works for the good of
those who love him. (Romans 8:28)

You intended to harm me, but God
intended it for good to accomplish
what is now being done, the saving
of many lives. (Genesis 50:20)

I'll see to it that everything works out for
the best. (Isaiah 54:17 THE MESSAGE)

We have a lot of questions, don't we? Will
the money come in? Will the tests turn
out right? Will I survive this round of layoffs?

Is there any way to stop this divorce? Is there any reason at all for hope?

It's easy to feel like a cork bobbing in a sea of uncertainty. We don't know where life is going to take us, so we wonder if anyone is in charge of history. In moments like that we have to turn to promises like this: In all things God works. And not only does he work, but he works for the good of those who love him.

The whole Bible is a demonstration of this promise, especially the Old Testament story of Esther. Maybe you've heard it before. It's the story of a man named Haman, who hated the Jewish people so much that he plotted to have them all killed and got King Xerxes of Persia to pass an irrevocable edict to make it happen.

But that was only one story line. God was writing another. He loves the Hebrew people, so he placed Esther, a Hebrew woman, as queen in the court of Xerxes.

Her cousin Mordecai urged her to speak to the king, to ask him to spare the lives of the Jews. Esther—afraid for her own life— reminded him that even though she was queen, she didn't have the privilege to saunter into the throne room of the king. In fact, if she approached without being summoned, she could be killed.

And her cousin said, "Do not think that because you are in the king's house you alone of all the Jews will escape. For if you remain silent at this time, relief and deliverance for the Jews will arise from another place, but you and your father's family will perish. And who knows but that you have come to your royal position for such a time as this?" (Esther 4:13–14).

You see, Mordecai knew that God would deliver his people. The question was not, Will God win? The question he posed to Esther was, Will you be a part of the victory?

This same promise applies to us. God's victory is certain. Perhaps you look around and feel as if there are evil plots intent on your destruction. Maybe you see irresponsible leaders like King Xerxes in your life. You wonder where this world is headed.

The promise of God—and the promise of the Bible—is *God will win the day*. God will have his way. Esther knew she could trust God with the outcome. She would do what she could and leave the rest to God. So she went to the king to plead for her people, saying, "If I perish, I perish" (Esther 4:16).

The stakes were high, but God's plans were higher. Esther approached her husband, and when Haman's plot was revealed, the king had him killed. But the irrevocable edict still stood. So the king added another decree—this time allowing the Jews to fight back against any Persian attacker. In a battle that lasted two days, more than seventy-five thousand Persians were killed, and the nation of Israel was saved.

Do you sometimes wake up with anxiety? Do you dread the day of the attack? Do you worry about what's to come?

Maybe you need a reminder that "we may throw the dice, but the LORD determines how they fall" (Proverbs 16:33 NLT). You and I are not in control. But the good news is that we have a good God. And this good God is up to something good.

In all things—even in the evil plot of Haman and the irresponsible leadership of Xerxes—God is at work. So do not lose hope. Do not give up. The story you're a part of is not the only story being written. In the right way at the right time, God will reveal the other story line.

This promise does not say that in *each* thing God works for good—no one would say that Haman's plot was good or that what King Xerxes did was good—but that God works *all* things together for good.

Whatever you face, whatever trials attack you, you can rest in the assurance that God is in control, and he will use all of it to write a story for your ultimate good.

A Prayer of Promise

Father, I know that you will win the day. Your plan is in motion, and your story is being told in every corner of the earth.

Forgive me when my hope flags because I cannot see you at work. Just as you did in Esther's time, you are writing story lines that I don't yet see. But I will trust in your promise. Give me strength to trust, especially when it's hard.

Help me do what is right, knowing that you alone are responsible for the outcome. In Jesus' name, amen.

Cleaned Up from the Inside Out

The Promise: God is at work in me.

It is God who works in you to will and to act in order to fulfill his good purpose. (Philippians 2:13)

I no longer live, but Christ lives in me. The life I now live in the body, I live by faith in the Son of God, who loved me and gave himself for me. (Galatians 2:20)

He who began a good work in you will carry it on to completion. (Philippians 1:6)

His divine power has given us everything we need for a godly life. (2 Peter 1:3)

Have you ever opened a refrigerator that's been unplugged for a week? It's an experience you'll never forget. Trust me. After a few days rotten food begins to decompose, giving off smells that you can't believe. Just cracking the door open will make your eyes water and your nose sting.

There's no denying it needs to be cleaned. Scrubbing the exterior, decorating it with designer magnets, or splashing it with expensive cologne is not going to make the inside of the refrigerator any cleaner.

Who in their right mind would think you could clean the inside by focusing on the outside? But we do it all the time.

Every human being on earth has some things inside that need to be cleaned out. Some of it comes from wounds. Some of it comes from mistakes. Some of the stink comes from decisions we've made or actions that were inflicted on us. Regardless of their origins, there are things inside each of us that we don't like.

When we try to clean the inside by changing the outside, we're missing one of the great promises of the Bible: God will change us in a miraculous way from the inside out.

The apostle Paul narrowed it down to one sentence: "The mystery in a nutshell is just this: Christ is in you" (Colossians 1:27 THE MESSAGE).

A Christian is a person in whom Christ is happening. It's somewhat of a spiritual heart transplant. The old heart is removed, and a new heart is deposited within. The old engine is removed, and a Ferrari engine is placed inside. Every element of Christ is supernaturally deposited into us when we give our hearts to Christ.

And this new presence of Christ in us undeniably changes who we are. That means it's not up to us to change ourselves, but we are to cooperate with the change that is already taking place.

The great story of the birth of Christ embodies this promise: what happened to Mary can happen to every believer.

Maybe you think the story of Mary is confined to Christmas pageants or midnight mass. But it's a story for every day because it's the story of Christ growing inside an everyday girl.

You probably remember how Mary was visited by an angel who told her she would have a child. But Mary didn't understand how that could be since she was a virgin.

"The angel answered, 'The Holy Spirit will come on you, and the power of the Most High will overshadow you. So the holy one to be born will be called the Son of God'" (Luke 1:35).

Mary could have said, "You have to be kidding me. That's not going to happen." But she didn't. Instead she called herself the servant of the Lord and said, "May your word to me be fulfilled" (Luke 1:38). And so it was that Christ was deposited into her.

I wonder what it was like to have Christ within her, growing and taking up more space, changing her interior until he was so big that he just had to come out. And she knew it was a miracle because she didn't do anything to make it happen.

Mary was just a normal person, but, oh, she's a reminder that God can do something great through normal people—like you and me.

The story of Mary and the virgin birth of Christ is a picture for us of what it means to have Christ within us. It's a supernatural deposit of Christ living in you and in me. When we accept Christ, every single one of his attributes is placed inside each of us.

This is cause for high optimism because

there are times when I don't like who I am. And there are probably times when you don't like who you are. Our response to that doesn't need to be a strange alteration to our outward selves or environment. Our response is to stand on the promise of Christ.

God is inside you, and he is changing you day after day, hour after hour. The presence of Christ is growing inside you so much that at some point he cannot help but come out. And what a difference it makes.

Can't forgive your enemy? Christ can, and he's inside you.

Need some self-control? It's already in you.

Can't face tomorrow? Christ can, and he is on the move in you.

The hope of Christ. The long-suffering of Christ. The kindness of Christ. The compassion of Christ. Every attribute of Christ is within you just waiting to come out.

If your insides feel messier than a forgotten refrigerator, lean on the promise that God is at work. He's cleaning you up, and he won't quit until your insides reflect exactly who is inside you.

A Prayer of Promise

Almighty God, I am humbled that you would choose to put your Spirit inside me. I am grateful for the work he is doing even now. Thank you for not leaving me a mess or asking me to clean up my own chaos.

I may not always understand the mystery of Christ in me, but help me to stand on this promise. When I am uncertain or confused, help me trust you as Mary did. "Let it be as you have said."

When I lack kindness, need patience, or struggle to forgive, remind me that Christ in me is everything I need for holiness. In Jesus' name, amen.

Bitter to Blessed

The Promise: Christ is my guardian-
redeemer, and his blessings are sure.

The LORD will redeem those who
serve him. (Psalm 34:22 NLT)

Praise be to the Lord, the God of Israel,
because he has come to his people and
redeemed them. (Luke 1:68)

In your unfailing love you will lead
the people you have redeemed.
In your strength you will guide them
to your holy dwelling. (Exodus 15:13)

The road to bitterness is a short one. One minute life seems great. Everything is going your way, and you might as well be singing the lead in a musical. You have no complaints. And then you lose what's most precious to you, and bitterness doesn't even wait for an invitation. It shows up on the doorstep of your heart and walks right in without knocking.

In the Old Testament book of Ruth, Naomi knew a thing or two about bitterness. In the span of five verses, she was forced to leave her home in Bethlehem because of famine, she lost her husband, and then both of her sons died. Everything she held dear was taken from her in just a few lines of the Bible.

Naomi was left with a broken heart, three graves, and two daughters-in-law. So she decided to return to Bethlehem. She tried to send her daughters-in-law back to their homes, but Ruth refused, saying, "Where you go I will go, and where you stay I will stay. Your people will be my people and your God my God" (Ruth 1:16).

So these two widows made the trip through the desert from Moab back to Bethlehem. Could there have been a more pitiful picture? Sagging shoulders. Sorrow-filled faces. Trudging steps.

Do you know that road? It wasn't a famine in Israel that left you bereft but a downturn in the economy. Maybe you didn't bury your husband and sons, but you had to bury your hopes and dreams. For whatever reason, you found yourself far from home and without hope. And you can understand exactly why Naomi did what she did next.

The name Naomi means *pleasant*, but when she reached Bethlehem, she changed her name to Mara, which means *bitter*. She was bitter at God, bitter at life, bitter at her circumstances. She'd been driven from her homeland by famine, driven back by death. She was discouraged and in need of a miracle. And wouldn't you know, a miracle appeared. His name was Boaz.

Boaz was everything that Ruth and Naomi were not. He was a man of means; they were women in need. He owned property; they owned nothing. He had workers; they needed work.

When we're bitter, when we're discouraged, when we're beaten down, we become sitting ducks for apathy. Lethargy kicks in, and that couch looks very comfortable. We begin to bathe in self-pity. Maybe that's where Naomi stayed, but not Ruth.

Ruth had every reason to be just as bitter as Naomi. But she had the wherewithal to say, "One of us needs to get to work." So she decided she would work in the fields, picking up the wheat stalks that had fallen to the side. There she placed herself in a position to be blessed.

The fields she worked in were owned by none other than Boaz. And when he saw her, he took notice. Maybe she was pretty. Maybe he was lonely. For whatever reason he asked about her. He spoke to her kindly. He protected her. He provided for her.

Redeemers behave in this way. They snatch the vulnerable out of trouble and protect the weak.

Ruth was so impressed with the kindness of Boaz that she rushed home to tell Naomi the story. And Naomi had a story of her own to tell: "That man is our close relative; he is one of our guardian-redeemers" (Ruth 2:20).

What is a guardian-redeemer? Well, during this time there was a law among the Jews that if a landowner died and had no sons, his property passed to his brother. And the brother was to marry his widow—or at least protect and provide for her. In this way the relative redeemed her from a difficult circumstance.

Hoping that Boaz would do that for Ruth and her, Naomi sent Ruth to him, and he was more than happy to care for them both.

By the end of the story, Naomi had a home, Boaz had a bride, and Ruth had a baby. And you and me? We have a reminder of exactly what Christ has done for us. We have no need for despair or bitterness. We have no reason to hang our heads or fall into apathy. We have a guardian-redeemer in Jesus Christ.

Boaz saw Ruth and Naomi's plight; Jesus sees your circumstance. Boaz was affluent; Jesus owns every square inch of the universe. Boaz spoke kindly; Jesus speaks to you with tenderness. Boaz told men to leave Ruth alone; Jesus commands Satan to leave you alone. Boaz gave Ruth water and bread; Jesus pours blessings into your life.

Because of Boaz, Naomi went from bitter to blessed. Because of Jesus, you can do the same.

A Prayer of Promise

Lord, you are my guardian-redeemer. You have rescued me from my circumstances and lifted my head. You speak to me with kindness and love. You see the situation that I face and have the power to take care of it.

Give me strength to battle against the

pull of bitterness. When I face difficult times, help me keep my eyes on you only. When I look at my hardships, it's easy to become so focused on myself that I don't see the work you've done.

If I've been stagnant or paralyzed by apathy or bitterness, give me a push in the right direction. I don't want to be bitter, so I choose to focus on your many blessings. Thank you. In Jesus' name, amen.

God Gets You

The Promise: I am assured that God
knows and understands me.

Our high priest is able to understand
our weaknesses. (Hebrews 4:15 NCV)

The Word became flesh and made
his dwelling among us. (John 1:14)

We have this hope as an anchor for
the soul, firm and secure. It enters the
inner sanctuary behind the curtain,
where our forerunner, Jesus, has entered
on our behalf. (Hebrews 6:19–20)

W e're only human." It's the cry of the
imperfect and the broken. It's a
recognition of failings, because we all fall short.
We do our best, only to stumble. We tumble

rounding first base and wonder if we'll ever make it home.

We've fallen in terms of morality, in terms of integrity, in terms of honesty. And we're left with broken hearts, broken dreams, and fading vision. We're mired in loneliness and drowning in discouragement. The distance between where we are and where we want to be seems impassable.

When we feel like that, we have promises like this: God understands.

How can God, who is all-powerful and all-knowing, possibly understand you? Well, God became one of us. God came to us in the flesh and form of Jesus Christ. He was both all God and all human, so he can understand.

And you and Jesus have a lot in common. Born to a mother. Acquainted with physical pain. Enjoy a good party. Rejected by friends. Unfairly accused. Offended by greedy religion. Unappreciated by siblings. Kept awake at night by concerns. Accused of being too rowdy. Dreaded death.

Jesus was born just as all babies are born, and his childhood was a common one. There's no evidence in the Bible that he was spared the awkwardness of adolescence. He may have been gangly or homely or even had pimples. We know he experienced weariness and hunger, sleepiness and grief.

You and Jesus do have a lot in common, and that's a big deal. He understands everything from small-town anonymity to big-city pressure. He's walked the pastures of the sheep field and the royal halls of a king. He's faced sorrow and death.

And he will face all of them again—*with you*.

The writer of Hebrews laid it out like this: "Our high priest is able to understand our weaknesses. He was tempted in every way that we are, but he did not sin. Let us, then, feel very sure that we can come before God's throne where there is grace. There we can receive mercy and grace to help us when we need it" (Hebrews 4:15–16 NCV).

Our high priest is Jesus Christ, and he understands our predicament so that when we come to him, he can give us just what we need when we need it. He doesn't wait on us with crossed arms and a wagging finger. He welcomes us with open arms and an extra helping of mercy and grace.

So, then, confidently approach him with your needs and requests, for you will find help. He doesn't leave you to languish in loneliness. When you fall, you're not forgotten. When you stumble, you're not abandoned. God gets you.

A Prayer of Promise

Heavenly Father, thank you. Thank you for understanding me. You sympathize with my weaknesses, see my failings, and love me anyway. Your goodness and compassion astound me.

I need help, and I boldly come to your throne with my requests, trusting that you will help me.

Thank you for mercy. Thank you for grace. In Jesus' name, amen.

Notes

1. M. J. Stephey, "A Brief History of the Times Square Debt Clock," *Time*, October 14, 2008, http://content.time.com/time/business /article/0,8599,1850269,00.htm.
2. Henry Blackaby and Richard Blackaby, *Being Still with God: A 366 Daily Devotional* (Nashville, TN: Thomas Nelson, 2007), 309.
3. Karl Barth, *Church Dogmatics*, vol. 4, part 1, *The Doctrine of Reconciliation*, trans. G. W. Bromiley, ed. G. W. Bromiley and T. F. Torrance (London: T&T Clark, 2004), 82.